MW01257803

TRANSVERSE

Poetry About Being Transgender

TransVerse by Jamie Winters

Second Edition

ISBN-13: 9781731271075

Cover by Ashwords Design

Dedicated to Dorothy

Without you, Theo wouldn't exist.
Thank you for sticking it out until
it got better.

TABLE OF CONTENTS

A NOTE

TO THE READERS

This book contains some graphic language about sex characteristics that may not be suitable for younger audiences.

This book also contains several poems about dysphoria—a state of unease or anxiety, in this case, over one's body—which may cause stress reactions in some individuals, such as those who experience dysphoria. For a list of poems by subject, please see the index at the back of the book.

These poems are based around my experiences as a transman—that is, someone who was given a female marker on their birth certificate, but later declared themselves to be male. I don't claim to know what it's like to be a transwoman, and my experiences are not representative of every trans person in the world. I have stayed as true to my story as I know how, but I am only one small piece of the puzzle. If you have someone trans in your life, please take the time to learn their unique story.

PREFACE

In the spring of 2016, I enrolled in a poetry class at college. This was in addition to the publishing class I was already taking that semester. I knew it was a writing heavy term, but I only had those two classes standing in my way before I was given a creative writing focus award, and I was determined to complete the requirements for the award before summer. I mostly took poetry because I needed a class in a discipline other than my fiction classes and poetry sounded the most interesting to me out of what was available. I had written poetry a little in my teens but had mostly given it up as I had gotten more and more involved in writing novels.

That class ended up reawakening a poetry spark in me, however. We talked about creating a vivid image in a writer's mind, and how to use the form of poetry to play and experiment with language in a way that I couldn't do with my prose writing. I remembered how apt poetry was for its ability to capture a single moment and feeling in time without the same problems that writing novels sometimes had. I fell in love with poetry all over again, for completely different reasons than why I loved prose. I started seeing poems everywhere, and ended up coming home several times with poems scribbled on scraps of paper, napkins, or one time, even my arm.

Meanwhile, I was nearing the end of term, and my publishing class was requiring a final term project. We were supposed to take prose and poetry we had worked on that year, and use it to create a small book that we were supposed to bind by hand and present to the class. I started scouring through my work in search of a common theme, and found that there was one part of my life that I kept writing about again and again: being transgender. It meant coming out to my classmates, but it was something that felt important to me. Several states were passing laws on trans people not being allowed to use the bathroom they identified with, and I felt it was a good time to share my part of the story. And besides, I couldn't find another theme in my writing from that term.

Thanks to my poetry class, most of the work I had was poems, though I also had a couple short stories about being transgender. I combined the work together, bound them into several copies of a book, and put some butterflies on the cover as a last minute thought.

After my class was over, I decided to give a last round of edits to the book and self publish it in June of 2016. I ran through it with another round of edits, put a last minute addition of "Frequently Asked Questions" in the back of the book, and got ready to finalize it for printing. At the time, the book was titled "TransForm."

Then the shooting at Pulse happened. On June 12, 2016, a man named Omar Mateen ran into a gay nightclub called Pulse and started shooting. 49 people were killed, and another 53 were injured. It was the deadliest mass shooting by a single shooter, and also the deadliest incident against LGBT people in US history. The LGBT community was distraught and terrified. Here we had thought there had been so much progress what with gay marriage being legal, but then there were LGBT people getting murdered, and some people even responding to the shooting saying they deserved it. It was terrifying, especially with pride parades around the corner and feeling like another shooter would pop out at any moment. I panicked and pulled back from my publishing schedule, saying I would publish once the commotion had died down and I felt safer.

While I was pulled back from the project, I decided I would take the extra time to make the book even better and give it another round of edits. I decided to give my FAQ section more consideration than just an afterthought and to make sure it actually adequately answered questions. I went to a writing group I'm a part of and asked them what they would ask a trans person if they could ask anything without seeming rude.

The response was so beyond what I had expected. The post blew up overnight, with me ending up answering questions non-stop for hours and hours. I was blown away. People really wanted to know that much about being trans? There was nowhere safe for people to get the answers to these questions?

After the dust had settled down, I typed up a list of questions for myself based on the thread, and found myself with several pages worth of questions to answer. I started writing out answers to the questions, though it was quickly becoming clear to me that the FAQ section of the book was easily going to become the largest section of the book, as well as being the section of the book that would actually sell the book. I kept writing, until I realized that these questions were becoming a book of their own, and I would do better just scrapping the poetry and short story portion of the book.

That got me depressed about working on the book for a while. I loved something that my poetry did that no amount of nonfiction could do. There was something about poetry that made me feel like I was giving people an actual window into what it was like inside my brain, even if that window only lasted long enough for one snapshot of my life. I kept writing more poems, no longer knowing what I was going to do with all of them, even though I loved them.

Then I was struck with sudden inspiration. Maybe my poems no longer fit in TransForm, but there were enough to easily make their own companion book of poetry. It meant that those who liked poetry could read the poems for further insight, and those who didn't enjoy poetry could skip it and read the Q&A book. It was the perfect compromise. I played around with other words that started with "trans," and eventually found the perfect one: TransVerse.

What you're holding in your hands now is my attempt to be true to that original vision I had when assembling TransForm for class. I even kept the butterflies that were part of the original. This book is very near and dear to my heart, and I'm so happy to finally be releasing it into the world.

If I'm honest, I'm also very scared about releasing this book. I'm terrified that the anger towards the LGBT community still hasn't calmed down enough. I've been seeing more and more hate crimes and angry things shouted in public at people. But I'm also a believer of the idea that hate comes from ignorance and a lack of understanding. Yes, there are some people in the world who may never want to learn or change their mind, but there are also a lot of people who are able and willing to change for the better when given the chance. I think it's part of the job of writers like me to make sure that those people have access to the information they need.

Every poem is like a snapshot of the soul, and when you gather as many together in one place as I have for this book, you can start to get a fairly clear picture of of a person's life. I've tried to arrange the poems in as chronological of an order as possible, so you can see the progression of my life, from the young girl in denial to the man I am today. Whether you're someone who wants to be a better ally, or someone who just had someone they love come out to them as trans, a trans person still grappling with their own feelings, or even someone who isn't sure how they feel about trans issues—you are welcome here. I hope this collection of snapshots gives you a chance to live in someone else's shoes for a moment and see things from a different perspective.

Be who you are
and say what you feel,
because those who mind
don't matter
and those who matter
don't mind.

—Theodor Seuss Geisel

trans•verse

(trans'vərs, tranz'vərs) v.t.

1. To overturn; to change.
2. To change from prose into verse, or from verse into prose.

PRE-TRANSITION

TEMPORARY REBELLION

Now in her dorm room, she
carefully budgets aside two dollars
and fifty cents every month

for the part of her they can't control.
Every Monday, she
slaps a new tattoo on

her neck,
counting to a minute,
whispering her weekly prayer.

She started with a butterfly
of every color, stretching
across her jugular, ripping

with her words of pride
every time someone sneered
"Is that real?"

By Sunday, the butterfly
was grey and stiff, a dry riverbed
of ink and glitter to be scrubbed with vinegar.

By Monday, a fairy rubbed against
the collar of her tye-dye t-shirt,
as if the butterfly never existed at all.

She thinks herself a rebel, unaware
that rebellion can't be bought
from a supermarket

with two quarters.

BROKEN

im   what
stuck   will
in   hap   pen
this   to
bro   ken   us
world   ?

why   or
cant   more
i   im   port   ant   ly
get   what
free   will
from   hap   pen
this   to
bro   ken
world   You?
?

ASSUMPTIONS

Sometimes,
you see someone from behind
with tight jeans
and long hair,
and it's clear they're a woman.
Until
they turn around
and you see the beard
and it's clear they're

not.

PINK STINKS

I don't like pink.
I don't care what you think.
I think the color stinks.

It's not the color that gets me, really.
But rather that it's girly.
Which makes me feel crappy.

Please don't give me another skirt.
I have no idea how to flirt.
I don't know why being a girl hurts.

So I'll tell you—
I'd rather something blue.
Because I thought you knew.

I don't like pink.
I don't care what you think.
I think the color stinks.

DYING TO KNOW

I'm dying to know
Tell me who I am
Tell me what I seek
Tell me, please tell me

What do you think of me?
Life's answers are out of my grasp
I don't know how much emptiness I can take
I need a purpose to define me, otherwise I can't
    be anyone
I don't know how I can live like this
Life's answers may never come
Is this who I'll always be?

Tell me, please tell me
Tell me what I seek
Tell me who I am
I'm dying to know

TWO FLOWERS

Two flowers stood near a lane
Their stems knotted together
Entwined for strength, but in pain
Braced for all kinds of weather

The Pink was shriveled and dry
The pink of her petals blurred
She appeared ready to die
If not for Blue beside her

The Blue was stronger and tall
Though his petals were quite torn
He too looked ready to fall
Looking so faded and worn

Together they stood as one
And where one flower would fail
They grew stronger in the sun
Bringing color to the trail

SLIPPING

I no longer know who I am
Always slipping, slipping
through my fingers like sand
I try to hold on,
I try to keep moving,
But there's still so many things I can't understand

IT MATTERS

"Gender doesn't matter."

Tell that to the child
who wished that she had been born without
    genitals
because they're stupid and gross
and completely meaningless.

Tell that to the teenager
who spent nights staring at her ceiling
trying desperately to disconnect
from her body.

Tell that to the young adult
who spent years telling everyone something was
    wrong
but she just didn't know why her
brain was malfunctioning.

Tell that to the man
who only just started to learn that none of
these things were normal to
feel growing up.

HIDDEN LIES

Life is
spinning lies
cloaked in pleasantry

Life is
hidden guilt,
hidden mistakes,
hidden sorrow

And sometimes
lies cannot be believed
even when
you pine for their sweet nothings

Truth
is always hidden
beneath fear and anguish

I know what I am
and unlike everyone else
I cannot hide from it

SECRETS

I have a secret

About something that keeps
Me up late at night.

Are you able to listen?

Because I need you to know,
Or I might lose my mind from
Years of hiding who I am.

META DATA

sitting up at
3 in the morning
writing poetry
hoping it fixes something
anything
oh please just
fix me if
i vomit
enough words on paper
will they stop
cluttering my brain
their inky arms tangling
around each other
until they change into
one giant black knot
of words
i don't know how to say

OTHER WORDS

"I love you" is a cheesy
way to start a poem, but
I don't have other words
to tell you

it's okay if
you don't look like yourself.
I can see
the real you, no matter what lies
your body tries to sell me. The real
you is the you
I fell in love with. But don't get scared
by that, because
you also need to know

it's okay if
you don't know who you are, because
I know your heart and
that will never change.
And neither will my heart and
its feelings for you. Because
that's what love is
and

I love you.

TRANSITION

LYING ON A SIDEWALK

Shattered pieces
of a mirror
Lying
on the sidewalk
each one reflecting
a different
part of me
hair
eye
nose
each one

wrong.

STUCK

I slide my hand into the crevice
between breast and chest,
slick with warmth and sweat.
I'm sure that if I grabbed
and pulled, it would separate
with a *pop*. Meanwhile
I would be stuck
holding a globe of fleshy
jelly.

Or maybe it would come off
with a *suck*. Like an
octopus pulling its tentacle
away from its prey,
the suction clinging until
the last second, leaving
a red circle
where boob used to be.

I'm so sure this is how
it would happen
that when nothing changes
I'm surprised.
Until I remember
this is my body—
whether I like it or not
—and I'm stuck.

Every night, I pause
between the mirror and bed
as if something will have
changed since the last time
I looked.

Every night, I tell
myself to keep wishing
one more night.

IDENTITY

When did you know
that your favorite food is ice cream?

Did you know
when the first bite of cold caressed
your tongue and
you closed
your eyes, reached out
to your mother and
begged for more?

Or.

Did you know
when you realized you were
counting pennies
for a trip
to the ice cream parlor with its blast of
air conditioned freedom—
the ability to sit in silence
and eat ice cream
with other people who love ice cream. Though
you only go once
a month, all you ever think about
is pennies
traded for bliss.

PUBLIC EYE

What am I to you?

Just another whiny millennial
looking for justification as to why
I'm a special snowflake?

Do you think I'm someone
who lies awake at night plotting
ways to get more and *more* attention?

Do you think being trans
somehow opens doors for me that I
couldn't open on my own?

Do you think
this helps me?

Despite the bullying?
        the stereotypes?
        the threats?
        the misery?
        the judgment?

If it's so great,
why don't you join me?

DID ANYONE TELL YOU?

Why must you crush your heart?
Why must you be in pain
Caused by your own hands?

You could have joy
If you chose your own path
You don't need to change much

Don't you know that
It's not weak to be happy?

THEODORE

Try on different names like clothing,
waiting
until one will finally sit up,
smack you across the face and say,
"Yes! It's me
you want to live with for the rest of your life!"

Kai
     Phoenix
          Edward
               Alexander

With each change, the name
rips off like velcro,
leaving you
red and tender all over. But
you keep trying new names,

hoping that one of these days,
one of them will actually
finally stick. And

when the right one finally comes along,
it's as if it was there
the whole time,
waiting,
and now it finally sits up and says,
"What took you so long?"

THE RED SOFA

Dysphoria is
going to the store to buy a black sofa,
but they give you a red one
and pretend it's the same.

When you go back to the store
to return it, they say
there are no exchanges or returns allowed. You
have to learn how to live with the red,

because it's just a color, and
it's not as if your sofa defines
who you are, so stop
making a big deal out of nothing.

You want to try and let it go,
but your entire living room is green, and
the red just looks garish
trying to be something it's not.

It's not that you hate red sofas,
because it really is a lovely sofa. But
every time you look and see the red, you
remember
the black sofa that was supposed to be there.

And you can't help but be sad
for something that will never be.

BOUND

pushing
squeezing
o u c h
b r e a t h e
s t a n d
t   a   l   l
s q u i s h
b r e a t h e
t i g h t
p r e t e n d
n o r m a l
b r e a t h e
o   u   c   h
f   i   n   e
s   a   f   e
n o r m a l
b r e a t h e
o   u   c   h
o   u   c   h
o   u   c   h
b r e a t h e
i   have
to   wear
c h a i n s
to   be
f   r   e   e

FIGHTING LIONS

There's no possible way to feel
the effects of testosterone
15 to 20 minutes
after your very first shot. But
I swear,
when I walked out of the clinic into
the sharp cold air,
I did. It was like
I had been fighting a lion for years
and the adrenaline finally wore off. Because
I started feeling achy
and tired
everywhere.
Like the battle was finally
over.

UNCOMFORTABLE

Just to let you know
It's okay if you're uncomfortable
I'm uncomfortable every day
We can be uncomfortable
Together.

ONE WING

One wing is not enough
I'm struggling to survive
I'm falling towards the ground
I know I'm going to die

I'm the boy with shattered reflections
And feathers beneath his feet
My clothes hide who I am
I march to a different beat

Maybe once I was an angel
But I'm not really sure
My body's slowly dying
To an illness of no cure

I've only got one wing
Was it ever once a pair?
I'm reaching for the heavens
But never getting there

BEING TRANS

Being trans is

Like having a beehive
Where your heart is supposed to go

Like having a radio tuned to two frequencies
Instead of a brain

Like having hands for feet
And feet for hands

Like having prickly velcro
Instead of skin to protect you

Like having sandbags draped over your shoulders
As if you were a balloon about to

Float away

Being trans is

Like having everything misplaced
Except no one ever believes you.

THE FIRST THREE
MONTHS

Second puberty is stranger than
the first, though you already know
what's coming.

Still, you can't help but be
surprised at your body
changing and morphing
into something—someone—different.

The voice cracks and drops.
The first chin hair grows in.
The armpit sweat becomes toxic nuclear waste.
The stomach becomes a screaming two year old.

And though it's the you
you've always pictured
—the you you want to be—
you can't help but feel distant
from your own body
still. Like you woke up in somebody
else's life, and any minute now,
the nightmare will be back.

YOU OUGHT TO KNOW

Before you come,
You ought to know
The name I use
Isn't the name I'm called
At home

HOW TO DEAL WITH DYSPHORIA

Sometimes it becomes a black hole
in the pit of my belly and
all I can do is
shove more things at it—

a manly photo,
compression wrapped around my chest like a
snake,
a sweaty sock safety pinned under my pants,
that "manly ruggedness" that comes from a day
without shaving

—trying to shut it up. Still
the black hole demands something,
anything,
to stop the voice in my head that whispers
"you're a girl."

REGIFTING

please oh *please*
Let's set up a gift exchange
—but for trans people.

You want boobs?
please
Take mine!
I insist.
Don't worry about it.
I wasn't using them
anyway.

Maybe in exchange,
someone else
might have a dick
for me.
And they'd say

"Someone gave it to me
years ago,
but I never liked it.
please
Take it!
Don't worry about it.
I don't want it sitting around
collecting dust."

please oh *please*

I wouldn't be picky.
As long as it was
mine
I would be happy.

SMUGGLING PADS

A man with a period is a
unique experience,
straddling the twilight zone
of gender.
No bathroom knows they need to
accommodate him,
so he's stuck smuggling in pads via his
back pocket,
hiding them in his hand to throw away on the
way out.
Watching and waiting for when the bathroom
is empty,
hoping no one will catch his
dark secret,
claiming his aspirin is for
a headache,
which it is, but also so
much more.

DON'T

Don't be small,
Take up space.
Don't squish your nonexistent balls.
Don't smile at strangers,
Nod at them instead.
Don't wave your hands around.
Don't let your voice slip high.
Don't flip your hair.
Don't giggle.
Don't turn when they say "miss."

I recite my rules in my head
over and over
every time I go out,
eyeing strangers from the corner of my eye,
wondering if they know.
Wondering if they hate me yet.

Please don't know.
Of course they know.
Please just let me get home safe.

FIVE STAGES OF SELF

No one tells you before you transition
that you end up going through
the stages of grief.
Maybe for your past self, or
maybe for the life you expected.
Either way, you grieve—

"No, I'm not really trans.
I'm just a tomboy
with anxiety
and depression
and PTSD.
But I'm fine.
I just need to try harder."

"The fact that there even is
gender standards is stupid!
Society is the only reason
I feel broken!
If I could just
be a hermit, then this would
all go away and not even be a problem."

"Okay, so I guess I like being a boy.
But if I only do it at home,
then maybe everything will be fine.
Just let this be a secret
and I'll do whatever at home
to keep myself sane.
Just don't make me come out."

"There's nothing I can do
to fix this. Not even
all the surgeries and hormones
in the world will make me
have XY chromosomes. And everyone
will want to kill me for even trying."

"If I don't find a way to live
the life I'm meant to live,
then I won't live a life at all. And
a life fighting for happiness
is a good life,
and I want it."

—and like all grief,
it hits you like a truck
because no one talks about it.

OPPOSITES COLLIDING

We'll always have the Qwik Mart
Where we ducked in through the rain
And you bought me strawberry soda
And strawberry malted milk balls
And the red starburst

I stood there with arms
Full of pink
As you searched
For your soda. And I remember
Thinking how we were
Two opposites colliding
In the same space
The transman and transwoman

Though we were more of
The transboy and transgirl
Sharing our second puberty
And sodas
And laughs
As if we were still in high school

I remember thinking
I would protect you from anyone
Who crossed us
And in that moment
I was you and you were me
Complete opposites
But
Exactly the same.

PLEASE ASK

I see you staring.
I hear you stammering.
I know you're struggling.

Seriously.
Just ask me.
"What pronouns do you prefer?"

I won't bite, promise.

WHEN YOU GOTTA

If I go in there,
I won't be safe.
I'll be naked, exposed,
and someone might be mad
at me for existing.

But I have to go.

The stubble means man,
but the period means woman.

If I choose wrong,
surely
everyone will know
as soon as they look at me.
Of course they know--
I can't hide anything.

There's nowhere for me.
Just cross your legs
tighter,
think about something else, and
hope for the best.

THE DYSPHORIA MONSTER

It lurks under the bed as
I crawl out in the morning
slithering like an oil spill
behind me
as I stumble through the dark house
and flick on the bright red glow
of the coffeemaker—a
single glowing eye watching me
stagger towards the bathroom.
The shadow slinks behind
me, wrapping around my ankle and
when I look up in the mirror,
there it is,
staring back at me as if
I could ever forget it was there.

Post-Transition

PRACTICE MAKES PERFECT

Just be Theo.
Stop being her; she's
gone now. Years of

practice pretending
to be someone I'm not
made it too easy to

not be me.

MY NAME

When you say my name,
Please don't spit it in my face
Like it's a disease.

I chose it with care
Like a mother for her child.
My name is precious.

Don't use my old name.
It's a piece of bad memories
I'd rather forget.

BECAUSE ENGLISH

Gender neutral parents must not exist
because English
doesn't have a word for them.

There are mothers and fathers
and mamas and papas
and mommies and daddies
and moms and dads,

but there are no words
for people who aren't
a mommy or a daddy,
so they must not exist.

Because English
has words for everything
that exists and don't you know
you can't make up words?

REINCARNATED

Sometimes, when he
lies awake at night, he
can remember his
life from before. Sometimes he
wonders if it was better when he
didn't know anything, as miserable as he
was through it all. At least then, he
didn't have memories of her haunting his
mind at night. At least then, he

didn't have to think about how she
had died without

him.

DAILY DECISIONS

I'm never comfortable.
Even at home, slouched
in front of the computer
wearing boxers and
a ripped t-shirt.

I thought I gave up
primping and preening
when I denounced my womanhood. But
now

every day is an agonizing decision:
pain of the body
or
pain of the spirit?

Do I stuff myself into
a box—flattening one area
while stuffing another with socks
until,
molded and pressed,
I resemble
expectations?

Or

do I give my body a chance
to breathe—my
boobs flapping
when I answer the door, my legs
pressed together,
trying to pretend
the void isn't there?

TRANSGENDERED

I don't even know what "transgendered"
is supposed to mean. Is it
a past tense form
of transgender?

   "Oh, back in the day, I *transgendered* quite a bit
                                          myself,
           but that's all behind me now."

Do you think you're saying
that this is some label I applied to myself
that has no actual basis
in reality?

   "Yeah, he totally *transgendered* himself last week.
               He'll never get that promotion now."

I'm just a transgender man—
no -ed required!
All you're doing is making it sound like
you don't English very well.

GUESS THEIR GENDER

I play a secret game with myself
Whenever I'm in public.
I call it "Guess Their Gender."
It's a horrible game.
I use my knowledge of being trans
to guess if anyone around me is trans—
if anyone is like me.

That man with the too-small hands.
Or the woman with the sharp nose.
Or the kid with the long hair and a flat chest.

Maybe they're trans.
Maybe they would understand
if I sat next to them and
talked about feeling out of place,
misgendered by strangers.

But what if I'm one of those strangers?

"Guess Their Gender" is a horrible game.
I hate it.
But I can't help but keep searching
for someone like me
who understands.

DENIAL OF SELF

I don't know
me.
I've changed since back then.
And yet we keep passing
each other.

I want the world to stop
spinning.

I can't see
me.
Waiting for me—but
I'm invisible to
me.

You don't know I'm
in pain.
I don't know
me.
I've changed since back then.

I don't know if I'll ever see
me.
Because I'm too stuck on
you.

I'm waiting for you, just
you.
Take my hand and let's fly
—let's ignore everyone
I am.

THE RIGHT CHOICE

Doubt likes to sneak up on me
In the middle of the night
In the shower
Eating lunch
Getting dressed
Have I made the
right choice?
No, but *really*.
How do you know
when something is the right choice
if everyone tells you
it's wrong?

Fear is never far behind doubt
Sticking me to my chair
Making my arms heavy
Cold fingers
Cold heart
Could it be true that
I'm wrong?
No, but *really*.
How can I tell the whole world
they're wrong about me
when it feels like sometimes
they might be right?

IN REVERSE

i hate
that you would trade e v e r y t h i n g
i've always wanted
for e v e r y t h i n g
i've worked so hard to dispose of.
but

i can't blame
you. i know
e x a c t l y
how you feel.

even though i feel it in
reverse.

HAVE YOU HAD THE SURGERY YET?

No, I haven't cut off
the meat sacks yet,
if that's what you're asking.
Not that it's any of your business, but
cutting off meat sacks is a lot more hassle
than one would think.

First I need money.
More money than I've ever seen in my life,
plus a couple thousand more.

Then I need letters written
verifying that I'm not doing this on a whim and
I know I can't go back.

(Because who *doesn't* want meat sacks?!)

Then I need consultation,
more consultation, and don't forget a year
long waiting list.

Then I need time off work,
which seems easy, except for the fact that
my co-workers don't know I'm trans.

(It also doesn't pay the bills.)

Finally, I need bed rest—LOTS of bed rest—and
hopefully a helper who can do anything
that requires me lifting my arms over my head.

So, not that it's any of your business,
but
it's going to be a *long* while
before the meat sacks are cut off.
Besides,

no one calls me ma'am anymore,
no one screams at me from their cars anymore,
no one knows now unless I want them to,
people are surprised when they hear I'm trans,
and
I'm not wishing I were dead anymore.

So what does a couple of meat sacks
have anything to do with it?

THEO AND I

Theo and I
Were almost two people
Sometimes
Where he was strong
I was weak
Where he was loud
I was quiet

But
In the ways that mattered
We were the same
When I cried
He cried
When I was scared
He was scared

When my heart cried out
In pain
As I stayed up all night
Tears streaming down my face
He was there
Next to me
His heart screaming
A duet to mine

Who was Theo?
He was me
Only so much more

FIGHTING vs. CONFORMING

Every morning
I need to make the decision
between being the real me
or the me the world understands.

Do I feel more like fighting
or conforming today?

Every piece of femininity I
drape over myself
calls my gender into question. Even though
it wouldn't if I had never
needed to abandon it in the first place.

WHEN I WAS YOU

I was you once,
long ago.

But now

I can't recognize
your face
your words
your memories

Sometimes we talk
I'm the alien
You're normal

You taught me
to shut up
to look down
to write

You're everything I hate
and love
about my past

I can't outrun you
I can't scream over you
I can't erase you

It's not fair
I'm stuck with you
when you tried so hard
to erase me.

FOR DOROTHY

You were my everything, back in the day.
No love would be better; no stars would shine
    brighter.
No matter the outcome, I never was swayed—
In battles of faith, I was always a fighter.
I once was so sure that you knew the way;
You would protect from a life full of sin.
Years later, I learned we had gone astray
And the truth I had known never had been.
You are my girl half I want to forget,
While I am the man that didn't exist.
But my heart forever is trapped in your debt
No matter how much I once was dismissed.
Because I must admit that this fact is true—
Despite all the hardships, I still love you.

Broken Puzzle

My name is Dorothy.
I can never be who I want to be.
Because then God will send me to hell
even if he still loves me.
I can't be anything else
I have to hide it
shove it under
hope and pray
if I shove it enough times
it will disappear.

Because I am broken.

This is not what humans are supposed to be
because I know this isn't God's will.
But shoving it under
is killing me slowly
and I don't even know why.
I know I am broken.
So why won't God fix me?

How many nights do I need to spend crying
days spent sleeping
just to avoid living
not eating
not playing
not loving.

My life will start when God fixes me.
Or my life will end if he doesn't
and he'll send me to hell anyway.
Because this is no way to live.

My name is Theodore.
A lot of people hate my choices.
But for the first time
in my life
I'm doing more than surviving.
Whether I hide myself
or not
they'll know
and they'll hate me.

God never fixed me
so he must not think I'm broken.

I'm tired of waiting for life to start.
I'm tired of waiting to die.
Damned to hell
for being trans,
damned to hell
for suicide.

God doesn't create
unsolvable puzzles.
Everyone is broken
everyone sins
everyone is His child
and I'm no different.

God doesn't make the broken whole,
he makes the broken *see*.
God loves me the way I am
no matter what.
So it's about time I did too.

INDEX

MORE INFORMATION

If someone you love is transgender:
http://www.glaad.org/transgender/allies

If you're an educator ally:
http://www.glsen.org/article/trans-and-gender-nonconforming-student-resources

If your child is transgender:
http://www.hrc.org/explore/topic/transgender-children-youth

If your parent is transgender:
http://www.colage.org

If you think you might be transgender: http://www.advocatesforyouth.org/publications/publications-a-z/731-i-think-i-might-be-transgender-now-what-do-i-do

For more resources, please visit:
http://www.transequality.org/

If you're a trans person struggling with suicidal thoughts, please remember that you're not alone. There are people out there who think you're great and want to help you. For a trans friendly lifeline, please call **866-4-U-TREVOR (866-488-7386)**, or visit **http://www.thetrevorproject.org/chat**

THANK YOU!

Thank you so much for reading *TransVerse*. I hope you enjoyed the book!

If you enjoy my poetry, I plan on releasing more poetry collections next month, along with other books along the way. There will also be a companion book to this one coming out this month that deals with all kinds of frequently asked questions about being transgender. If you'd like to keep up with my new releases, you can join my mailing list at **http://eepurl.com/dwWXoH.** I only use email to communicate about book news, promise.

And if you have a moment, please consider leaving a review at Amazon or Goodreads. As an author, I love looking through reviews to see what my readers have enjoyed and what I could improve on. And as a reader, I love looking to reviews for advice when I'm trying to find a new book to enjoy. Reviews are a great way to help keep our book community connected!

Thanks again for reading, and I hope to see you around again in the future!

–Jamie Winters

IF YOU LIKED TRANSVERSE...

Check out the companion book, *TransForm*!

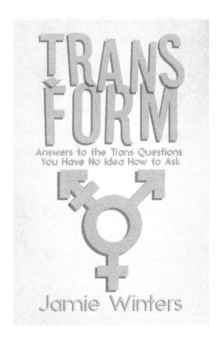

Do you need a lifeline when it comes to transgender topics?

Navigating through conversations about trans subjects when you're still a newbie is terrifying. Do you sound like an offensive simpleton? Which pronouns should you be using when? What do all these new words even mean?

Consider this book your trans friend willing to answer any question you have, no matter how offensive. There's even a glossary in the back to help you navigate through conversations! In clear, simple language, you'll learn things such as:

• What it's like to transition and live as a trans person
• How to understand your own identity
• The difference between sexual orientation and gender identity
• What's considered rude and polite in the trans community
• How to come out or respond to a loved one coming out

Written by a trans man who spoke at a TEDx event on gender identity and how it relates to finding yourself, TransForm is meant to be a reference for all. Whether you're trans yourself and not sure where to start, someone who just learned someone they love is trans, or even if you're just wanting to be a better ally, you'll want to keep this book nearby for all your questions.

https://mybook.to/transform

ABOUT THE AUTHOR

Jamie Winters is a cat. You would think a cat can't be an author, but that's where you would be wrong.

Or at least, that what we say because it's easier. Blame it on our obsession with cats. Jamie Winters is actually a pair of co-authors who spent so much time writing together that they ended up getting married. After that, the natual next step was to start sharing a pen name.

Both the authors who make up Jamie Winters are somewhere outside of the gender binary. One of them is an AFAB trans man who has been transitioning since 2013. The other is a non-binary enigma. This book was written primarily through the perspective of the trans man, Theo, with enigmatic moments still sprinkled throughout.

If you would like to keep up with Jamie Winters' journey, you can follow him online at **https://jamiewintersauthor.wordpress.com/**. You know, whenever he gets a moment away from that darn needy human of his.

ALSO BY JAMIE WINTERS

i'm fine.
A Haiku Collection About Mental Illness

words can't describe this
feeling of bricks on my heart
so i say "i'm fine."

https://mybook.to/imfine

The Reluctant Dreamer
A Poetry Collection

Learning to trust is hard.
Learning to trust in dreams is harder.
Learning to trust in dreams despite a lifetime
of pain is practically impossible.
But it may be the most important thing you
ever do.

https://mybook.to/thereluctantdreamer